Maine Coon Cats

Jennifer Quasha

The Rosen Publishing Group's
PowerKids Press™
New York

For Katiana and Mimi

Published in 2000 by The Rosen Publishing Group, Inc.
29 East 21st Street, New York, NY 10010

First Edition

Book Design: Michael de Guzman

Photo Credits: pp. 1, 4, 7 © Renee' Stockdale/Animals Animals; pp. 8, 12 © Sydney Thomson/Animals Animals; p. 11 © Robert Pearcy/ Animals Animals and © Archive Photos; p. 15 © Robert Pearcy and Joe McDonald/Animals Animals; p. 16 © Ulrike Schanz/Animals Animals and © Archive Photos; p. 19 © Reed - Williams/Animals Animals; pp. 20, 22 © Robert Pearcy/Animals Animals.

Quasha, Jennifer.
    Maine coon cats / by Jennifer Quasha.—1st ed.
        p.   cm. — (A kid's cat library)
    Includes index.
    Summary: Relates the history of one of the oldest breeds of cats to develop in the United States and describes its physical and other characteristics.
    ISBN 0-8239-5510-9
    1. Maine coon cat—Juvenile literature. [1. Maine coon cat. 2. Cats.]   I. Title. II. Series: Quasha, Jennifer. Kid's cat library.
SF449.M34Q37 1999
636.8'3—dc21
                                                                                                98-53565
                                                                                                     CIP
                                                                                                      AC

Manufactured in the United States of America

Contents

This Maine coon kitten will grow up to be a loving pet.

The Maine Coon

The Maine coon cat is a large cat with long fur and a full, bushy tail. Maine coons are one of the oldest **breeds** of cats to develop in the United States. Maine coon cats first lived in New England, especially in the state of Maine. This is one of the reasons it is called a Maine coon cat. The other reason it is called a Maine coon is because it looks a little bit like a raccoon. Sometimes raccoons are called "coons." Maine coon cats and raccoons are about the same size and they both have dark stripes around their bushy tails.

5

What Does It Look Like?

The Maine coon has a large body that can sometimes weigh as much as 30 pounds. Maine coons are one of the largest breeds of cats in the world. Females are usually smaller than males. The Maine coon's fur is long and silky. It falls smoothly around the cat's body. The fur can be many colors, including brown, gray, reddish, or **tabby**. The Maine coon has a medium-sized head and large, **expressive** eyes.

The ears and feet of the Maine coon have tufts of fur around them. ▶

Cat History

Cats became pets to humans about 5,000 years ago in ancient Egypt. The people in ancient Egypt **worshipped** cats. They thought that cats were almost like **gods**. When wealthy or important people died, they were often buried with cats.

Throughout history, cats have been part of people's lives. Early **settlers** in America found that the large, fluffy cats in New England were very good at catching mice and rats. Soon these people saw that Maine coons were good **companions** as well as good hunters.

◄ *Today, more people in the United States have cats for pets than any other animal.*

The Maine Coon in America

Cats were first brought to the United States in the 1700s. They came on European ships. Cats were always welcome on ships because they would eat the mice and rats on board. If cats didn't catch the mice and rats, the mice and rats would eat the sailors' food.

When sailors came ashore, so did the cats. Some cats were left behind and had to hunt and live in the wilderness. The biggest, strongest cats with long fur were the only ones to survive the cold winters in New England. These **hardy** cats were the first Maine coons.

Sailors not only liked Maine coons because of their hunting skills, but because they were nice, friendly pets. ▶

Skilled Hunters

Early Maine coons had to hunt for their food, so they became very good hunters. Early settlers kept many of these cats around their barns and houses to catch mice and rats. Maine coons spent a lot of time outside and needed to stay warm. They developed special fur, just for that purpose. The fur grew longest on the Maine coon's belly. That's because the cat crawled very low to the snowy ground as it **stalked** its **prey**. Long fur on the belly would keep the cat warm. The Maine coon cat can also puff up his fur to make him look bigger and scarier to his enemies.

◀ *Maine coons are known for being one of the best mousers of all breeds of cats.*

Meow Myths

There are many **myths** about how the Maine coon cat came to be. A myth is a story that people make up to explain something that they can't explain any other way. One myth is that a cat brought to the United States on a ship **mated** with a raccoon. However, this could never happen. Scientists have found that it's not possible. The **genes** of a raccoon and the genes of a cat cannot be mixed. Though it is true that the first Maine coons developed from cats that came to America by boat, they are not related to raccoons.

Though they may look alike, we know today that Maine coons are not related to raccoons. ▶

Cat Tales

Another myth is that a sea captain named Coon brought the long-haired cats to the United States on his ship. According to this myth, Maine coons got their name from the captain.

There is even a myth about Marie Antoinette. She was the Queen of France in the 1790s. Just as the **French Revolution** was starting, she wanted her cats taken to the United States for safety. According to this myth, it was her cats that were the earliest relatives of the Maine coon.

Marie Antoinette was very fond of her long-haired cats and wanted to make sure they were protected.

Award-winning Cat

In 1895 the first all-breed cat show took place in Madison Square Garden in New York City. A brown tabby Maine coon named Cosie won the Best of Show, which is the highest award in the whole show. As her prize she got a silver collar and a silver medal. This was the first time that a Maine coon won such a high award. After this the Maine coon was the most popular long-haired cat in the United States. That lasted until the 1930s, when **Persian** cats began to gain popularity.

Even though Persian cats are now America's favorite long-haired cat, Maine coons such as this one are still very popular pets. ▶

Maine coons are very curious cats.

A Unique Cat

The Maine coon is **unique** in a number of ways. Unlike many other long-haired cats, the Maine coon's fur will not get tangled. Though it is long, it is smoother and easier to care for than the fur of other long-haired cats, such as the Persian.

The Maine coon is also known to make high-pitched chirping sounds. Nobody is sure why they do this. It could be to **attract** birds and mice for the cat to eat. It could also be just for attention. Either way, it makes this cat very special.

Gentle Giants

Maine coons are often called "gentle giants." This is because they are larger than many other cats. They also have a very gentle personality. They love to sit with their owners and are great with children. Maine coons are known to curl up and sleep in tiny spaces that seem too small for them. Some people believe that this goes back to their days on ships. The only places for cats to sleep on a ship were often very tiny. No matter where a Maine coon sleeps, it seems to bring happiness to the people around it.

Web Sites:

http://www.fanciers.com
http://www.hsus.org/catfact.html

Glossary

attract (uh-TRAKT) To cause other people, animals, or things to want to be near you.

breed (BREED) A group of animals of the same kind.

companion (kum-PAN-yun) A person or animal who spends a lot of time with another person.

expressive (ek-SPREH-siv) Full of meaning and feeling.

French Revolution (FRENCH REH-vuh-LOO-shun) A time of very important change and fighting that began in France in 1789.

gene (JEEN) A tiny part of cells that an animal gets from its parents. A gene tells the cells how the animal's body will look and act.

god (GOD) A being or object that is thought to have more power than humans.

hardy (HAR-dee) Strong and healthy.

mate (MAYT) A special joining of the male and female bodies. After mating the female may become pregnant.

myth (MITH) A story that may not be true.

Persian (PER-zhin) A type of long-haired cat.

prey (PRAY) An animal that is eaten by another animal for food.

settler (SET-ler) A person who moves to a new land to live.

stalk (STAWK) To follow something closely and secretly.

tabby (TA-bee) A striped and spotted pattern on a cat's fur.

unique (yoo-NEEK) One of a kind.

worship (WER-ship) To pay great honor and respect to something or someone.

Index